T0117675

emotional intelligence for couples

Simple Ways to Increase the
Communication in Your Relationship

emotional intelligence for couples

Simple Ways to Increase the Communication in Your Relationship

JOHN LEE

TURNER

Turner Publishing Company

445 Park Avenue • 9th Floor
New York, NY 10022

200 4th Avenue North • Suite 950
Nashville, Tennessee 37219

www.turnerpublishing.com

Emotional Intelligence for Couples:
Simple Ways to Increase the Communication in Your Relationship

Cover design by Mike Penticost

Library of Congress Cataloging-in-Publication Data

Lee, John H., 1951-
 Emotional intelligence for couples : simple ways to increase the communication in your relationship / John Lee.
    p. cm.
 ISBN 978-1-59652-828-4
1. Emotional intelligence. 2. Man-woman relationships--Psychological aspects. 3. Men--Psychology. 4. Emotions. I. Title.
 BF576.L444 2011
 152.4086'55--dc22
                         2011015176

Printed in the United States of America
11 12 13 14 15 16 17—0 9 8 7 6 5 4 3 2 1

This book is also available in gift book format as
24 Things to Increase the Emotional Intelligence of Your Man
(978-1-59652-739-3)

For my wife, Susan Lee

I've learned that people will forget what you said, people will forget what you did, but people will never forget how you made them feel.

~ Maya Angelou

Contents

Acknowledgments

I thank Todd Bottorff and all the folks at what I consider to be one of the best publishers in the business—Turner Publishing. The individual time, support, and energy that is given to writers is truly "old school," which for me works great.

I want to thank my very talented wife, Susan Lee, who edits everything I write so I won't look so bad to the good folks at Turner when they see what they think is my final draft.

I want everyone reading this to know that were it not for people like Bill Stott, Dan Jones, Robert Bly, Karen Blicher, Connie Burns, Vijay Director, Terry Allen, the men who put "men" in our little community of Mentone, Alabama, and my clients, workshop participants, and so many others, I would not have been able to write anything at all.

Introduction

After twenty-five years of counseling people and presenting workshops and working with hundreds of couples, I discovered early on that what most women want and pray for is that the men in their lives be more emotionally present and available, and not be afraid to deal with emotions and feelings, regardless of who is experiencing and expressing them.

By reading, applying, and practicing these 24 principles and tips, you and your spouse, lover, or significant other will experience greater intimacy and become more emotionally present and available to each other. Your communication will be clearer and more loving, and you will enjoy a deeper connection than you have ever known.

Feelings are as important as facts

First things first—a feeling is a fact at the moment a woman is experiencing it. Another fact: most women tend to be more in touch with their feelings and emotions than most men. Men, if you are reading this, emotion is as important as logic and reason. In other words, if a person—whether man or woman—feels sad because their pet of ten years is lost or has died, the sadness is as real as the sun, and they are not to be talked into suppressing their feelings. Instead, they should receive empathy. If someone is angry about losing a job, their anger is as real to them as the ground they are standing on.

Unfortunately, many people, particularly men, have been taught that expressing their feelings and emotions makes them weak or inferior in some way. Dr. Michael Rovito says, " . . . the forces that defined masculinity have therefore shaped and molded an idea of a man as one who should not demonstrate vulnerability or weakness in any kind of visible form." He continues to explain that a vulnerable man risks losing his masculinity. This perception is changing rapidly for younger generations who are being exposed to the concept of emotional intelligence early on in their education. As the singer/songwriter Bob Dylan said a long time ago, "The times they are a-changin.'"

It is time for men to stop shutting down their feelings and emotions and stop shutting down the women who, to a much larger degree, are not only in touch with their feelings but need to express them. It is time for men to open up and tell the women they love how they really feel, not just what they think.

This book provides both women and men with several takeaways. One is that you will increase your emotional literacy, vocabulary, and range. You will also increase and elevate your EQ (emotional quotient, or emotional intelligence quotient). You will use exercises in the book that will make you a more emotionally available partner, parent, or spouse and allow you to be more intimate and feel more connected to those you care about. At the same time, you'll be better equipped to succeed as a boss, employee, colleague, and friend.

During the last decade, high emotional intelligence has become a key factor in achieving success in everything from romantic relationships to a corporation's bottom line. Each day we make literally hundreds of decisions that require us to be in tune with our emotional selves—decisions that can't be made through reason alone. According to Daniel Goleman, author of *Emotional Intelligence: Why It Can Matter More Than IQ* (Bantam, 1995), emotional intelligence provides "the ability to sense, understand, value and effectively apply the power and acumen of emotions as a source of human energy, information, trust, creativity and influence."

In the recent past, a person's IQ (intelligence quotient) was the standard qualifying factor used to hire corporate executives or others filling high-power positions. It is now becoming secondary to a person's EQ. Studies show that a person's IQ is set by age twenty or twenty-one, but emotional intelligence can be increased any time and at any stage in a person's life.

EQ is rapidly becoming more important when it comes to hiring a manager or picking a mate because, as many of us have experienced, a high IQ does not equal happiness or success, whereas a high EQ is more likely to lead to happiness and success.

In an interview with the Chicago Booth News, Jamie Dimon, Chairman and CEO of JPMorgan Chase, said, "It's not IQ that leads to success. EQ is more important: emotional intelligence, social skills, how you relate, can you get things done. That's what makes a difference, especially in management."

All of what is said here is very applicable to your own emotional well-being, but *Emotional Intelligence for Couples* will also become a handbook to help the man or woman you love become more and more comfortable with their feelings and yours, at home and at work.

1
Establishing boundaries: taking the first step to increase emotional intelligence

1

And this is one of the major questions of our lives: how we keep boundaries, what permission we have to cross boundaries, and how we do so. —A. B. Yehoshua

Creating good boundaries

Whether you are a man or woman, it is imperative for safety to be a precondition for feeling and expressing emotions appropriately, and therefore, enhancing your EQ. A good starting point to increase your feelings of being emotionally safe is to take to heart a famous line by Robert Frost, "Good fences make good neighbors." Boundaries, if created and defended appropriately, will not only make you feel safe, but they will also help keep you from being overwhelmed by your own and other people's emotions. Boundaries are what will keep you and others safe to feel whatever you need to feel at the moment. This is because you will not feel violated, offended, abused, or exhausted nearly as often. The boundaries will enhance and clarify communication and emotional connection to those you care about or work with.

Boundaries are lines that you draw in the sand, on the carpet, in the air, in your soul, in your body, and in life in general. These are lines that others can't cross without re-percussions. A boundary is not imaginary even though you may not be able to see it. It says, "This is how close you can come to me—physically, emotionally, spiritually, financially, sexually, and verbally."

Before boundaries can increase emotional intelligence, you need to accomplish a few things first:

- Define boundaries.
- Discuss the different kinds of boundaries that exist.
- Understand your boundary errors.
- Explain boundary violations.
- Identify boundary impairment.

Building boundaries and tearing down walls

First, a boundary is not a wall. Walls are put in place by people who cannot establish boundaries or do not know how to establish boundaries. We can tell the difference be-tween a boundary and a wall by looking at our family and friends to see whether they have flat heads from banging them against our walls or calluses on their hands from trying to tear them down. Many of us know more about wall construction than boundary building.

Boundaries help us to separate our thoughts and feelings from those of other people, including but not limited to our parents, children, spouses, or friends. Boundaries help us figure out who we are and who we aren't. They show us where we begin and end, and where someone else begins and ends, by establishing the appropriate psychological, emotional, and physical space between us.

What boundaries do

Boundaries regulate distance and closeness and can be placed around:

- Our physical being
- Our emotional lives
- Our sexuality
- The words people say to us
- Our finances
- Our spirituality (and how to protect it)

Examples of boundaries

Emotional boundaries include how much of someone's anger, sadness, fear, or joy you will allow before you have had enough or become overwhelmed. These emotional boundaries say, *Your anger or fear is yours, not mine,* and vice versa.

Sexual boundaries, when in place, can communicate it is alright for someone to hold your hand, but that is all. They can put their arm around you but go no further. A person cannot talk about your sexuality or talk to others about your sexual habits or preferences. No one can touch your children sexually, and so on.

Informational boundaries help you draw the line when you have had enough information about this or that subject or person. You don't want to hear or take in any more because you may get overstimulated.

Financial boundaries will allow you to determine what you are willing to discuss financially, and with whom. Maybe you will talk to your boss about how much he pays you. You may talk to your father about what you paid for your home. Your accountant and banker will have greater access to your financial life, but you don't tell acquaintances or social friends about your financial life.

Spiritual boundaries determine what comes into your spiritual being. You may let your minister, priest, rabbi, or imam talk to you and give you spiritual advice, solace, or comfort, but not the person pounding on your door who wants to lay out their religious strategies or dogma.

One of the reasons it is important to establish good, clear boundaries is that they can be highly effective in dealing with and negotiating stress, anxiety, conflicts, confrontation, and intimacy. Boundaries can reduce tension, friction, and misunderstanding. They also, believe it or not, can increase connection and comfort. If you know where you begin and end and I know where I begin and end, we don't have to worry about encroachment, abandonment, invasion, or oppression.

Caution

A word of caution: as with any new tool in your emotional toolbox, the first time you use your boundaries and limits around unhealthy people, they will often react negatively. They may get very angry—even enraged or outraged—with you and try to talk you out of using your new psychological and emotional equipment for managing your life better. "You are just putting walls up between us," "Why are you not allowing me access to these parts of your life like you used to?" "You are becoming rigid." And in your early practice of setting good boundaries, you may doubt your ability to create healthy boundaries and even question yourself: "Am I being too inflexible?" "Are these really walls, not boundaries?" Very often, your boundaries may be a little over-the-top in the beginning because you have gone from no boundaries to all boundaries all the time.

2
Stopping boundary errors and violations from occurring

2

Take the trouble to stop and think of the other person's feelings, his viewpoints, his desires and needs. Think more of what the other fellow wants, and how he must feel.
—Maxwell Maltz

Boundary errors

Before you defend your boundaries, you must recognize through either boundary violations or boundary errors (terms coined by author Anne Katherine) when your boundaries are not honored.

Let's focus on the lesser offense of boundary error before we take on boundary violation. A boundary error occurs when there's a lack of information or miscommunication about cultural or social norms and customs. It is not intentional or malicious. And it often occurs because of lack of forethought.

Jennifer doesn't like to be kidded or teased about her premature grey hair. She's only twenty-one. Still, she gets unsolicited comments and "cute remarks" about her hair all the time. This would be a boundary error because she never told those making the comments that she wasn't comfortable hearing them. Talking too loudly with someone—error. Giving someone a hug without asking and then being told they don't like to be hugged by strangers—boundary error.

Boundary violations

An example of a boundary violation is when someone knows that Jennifer doesn't like to be teased about her hair but they do it anyway. Being told that their talking volume is too loud and persisting anyway—violation. Having been told someone doesn't like to be hugged by strangers but the stranger continuing to push that person to do so—violation. Of course, there are much more serious violations than the above examples, but you get the picture.

How do you know when a boundary violation has taken place if you are not familiar or comfortable with your and others' boundaries?

Feelings and signs that your boundaries have been violated

- Anger
- Betrayal

- Fear
- Shame
- Powerlessness
- Sadness
- Anxiety
- Unsafe feelings

These feelings say someone has gotten closer to you—whether physically, sexually, emotionally, or in another way—than you are comfortable with. Or they may reveal that someone has invaded your privacy, and you are not safe with that person doing so.

These signs and feelings can be identified as they are occurring, but ideally, it is best to identify them before it's time to defend your boundaries. Doing so will minimize or even eliminate many of the uncomfortable feelings associated with boundary violations.

If you can't defend your boundary, you may find yourself keeping your distance from the person or group you are letting cross it, or you may keep them at a distance with your wall of unavailability.

3
Defending your boundaries

3

I think one's feelings waste themselves in words; they ought all to be distilled into actions which bring results.
—Florence Nightingale

A boundary that isn't defended isn't a boundary

An important part of setting good boundaries is being able to stick with them and appropriately defend them when necessary. A few months ago I was teaching a workshop on boundaries and limits. About three hours into the presentation, after hearing me say for the third or fourth time, "A boundary that can't be defended is not a real boundary but just a really good idea," Tom raised his hand and said, "I set good boundaries with my mother when I go to see her, but she refuses to acknowledge them. But it's not because I don't have them, she just ignores them."

"Then they're not really boundaries," I explained, "because real boundaries can't be ignored. Think of the fence around your house. If you don't open the gate or tear down the fence, or if you don't let your neighbor tear it down, then your neighbor can't come into your space. Do you agree?" I asked him.

"No, I don't. Let me give you a personal example, and you'll see what I mean. I set a boundary and she ignores it, and then I get very angry. Well, no—to be honest, I get enraged. See, I go over for dinner every Sunday. She's all alone now that my father is dead. We sit down and I put on my plate what I want, and then she puts food on my plate that she wants me to eat, like brussels sprouts, which I hate. I tell her I don't want them and I don't want her to put food on my plate, that it's my plate!" He paused.

"So then what happened?" one of the workshop participants asks.

Tom continued his story. "She puts the food on every time. I set a boundary and she ignores it every time, so it's not that I don't make boundaries clear."

I asked this man, who owned his own auto repair shop, how old he was.

"I'll be thirty-two next month. What has that got to do with anything?" You could hear the irritation in his voice. "What do you want me to do?" he said, his face red with anger, "Throw the food in her face? She's my mother for Christ's sake."

"No, that would be rage, not defending a boundary."

Another workshop participant offered this suggestion. "How about saying something like, 'Mom, if you keep putting food on my plate, I'm leaving.'"

From all the nodding in the room, I could tell most of the workshop participants liked that idea, but it wasn't the right choice, either. "No, that's a threat," I said.

Highly emotionally intelligent people find many ways

Most of the people I've worked with over the years who have boundary issues tend to think there are really only two ways to defend a boundary. One is to leave the person who ignores the boundaries, and the other is to do something like what Tom said: "Throw the food in her face" or some other violent or aggressive act.

So what would be a good way for Tom to defend his boundaries with his mother? Next time he speaks to her, he could say, "Mom, I won't be coming over for Sunday dinner anymore. I'll be coming over on Sunday afternoon for tea only." Or, "Mom, I've already eaten, I'll sit here and watch you eat." If she asks him why, he can answer, "When I'm eating with you, I don't feel respected."

There are other options than just fight or flight, but

Tom's vision was clouded, and obviously his issue with his mother was long-standing.

Saying "no"—a great boundary word

If you don't desire to use walls, what do you do? You learn to say and mean the following words that many people almost never say (and mean) but perhaps only a few times in their lifetime: "No!" "No more!" "Enough!" "Stop!"

"No" is a complete sentence. The famous (or infamous) Gestalt therapist Fritz Perls said, "If you can't say 'No,' then your 'Yes' doesn't mean a damn thing." This type of person is constantly playing the role of the "Yes" man or woman to the detriment of his or her own physical, emotional, and spiritual well-being. Why is it so difficult to say something such as, "Stop," "I don't want to hear any more," "No more!" or "Enough!"? Because most who can't say these words regress to a time, usually in childhood, when these words were not allowed, or when our primary role models could not use them successfully and without negative consequences.

There are other ways to stop and defend boundary violations, encroachments, and invasions:

- Identify the specific violation: "When you don't knock before coming into my room . . ."
- Tell the person how you feel to not have your space, needs, and feelings respected: "I get angry and scared . . ."

- Add energy, body language, and sterner words: "I'm serious about this," while putting up your hand in a stop motion or planting your feet firmly.

Know what you will do and won't do should the violation occur again. However, it is very important that you don't tell the offender what the consequences will be. If you verbally convey the consequences to that adult, they will likely interpret your words as a threat or ultimatum. However, you do tell children what the consequences will be if they violate or disregard your boundaries so they can learn to make healthy choices in the future.

4
Knowing your limits

4

You get what you tolerate. —John G. Agno

Limits are even more of a mystery than boundaries. Even professionals confuse boundaries with limits—if they discuss them with their clients at all. In a nutshell, a boundary says, "This is how close you can come to me." A limit is the emotional and intellectual knowledge of how far you'll go with a situation with a marriage, job, parent, or child.

Posting your limits

Many people have trouble knowing what their limits are in both personal and professional circumstances. Mildred, a very compassionate and thoughtful mother and owner of a resale clothing store, called me very upset and angry. "I'm so angry with my son I don't know what to do," were the first words after "Hello." "I told him I would put him through two alcohol and drug treatment programs, and then he's on his own."

"How is that going?" I asked.

"Not too well. That is why I'm so mad at him. I have now put him through four of the best and most expensive treatment centers in the country."

"Mildred," I said, "What are your limits?"

She fired back, "I said two. But obviously it wasn't. That's why I'm so angry."

"So you don't know your limits and you're angry with him because he doesn't know them either?"

Mildred laughed and said, "Oh!"

Setting limits can actually lead to a deeper connection to those we care about. Because we don't know our limits, we go much further than or stop very short of where we want to be and how much we want to do with or for someone.

Not knowing our limits can turn us into caretakers instead of caregivers. Caregivers have good boundaries and know their limits. Caretakers go way beyond where they really want to go. Caretakers actually end up taking something out of those they are around—like their integrity, energy, self-esteem, or the money they find underneath the cushions of the couch or lying around. In other words, they have to take something for giving up something of themselves that they really do not want to give. Many people who don't know or pay attention to their limits tend to feel resentment and therefore feel they need some kind of payment or restitution. People who know and respect their own limits can care for others without resentment, without feeling like something is being taken from them, and they actually feel energized by giving to others. This is what I call being compassionately assertive, which I'll explain more about later.

When we listen to our own internal rhythms for closeness and separateness in terms of intimacy, interaction, or engagement, we know what our limits are. If we stay true to our rhythms, we know how long we can visit our parents without falling into old, destructive conversations and patterns. If we know when to seek solitude to recharge our batteries, then we won't have to push people away or run away from a relationship just because we can't say, "I need some time alone."

I asked another client of mine we'll call Terry, who was taking a sabbatical from interacting with his father, how long he thought he could be with him when he resumed the relationship before feeling overwhelmed. "Maybe thirty minutes, and then I'll become his little boy again who stays much longer with his daddy, and we'll be in the same old dysfunctional drama we're always in."

"How about staying just thirty minutes or less if that is your limit?" I asked.

"We'd probably enjoy each other's company. I'd leave on a good note because I'd still be an adult instead of a pissed-off kid who didn't want to ever come back or see his father for a long time."

Further purposes of limits

Limits not only help us establish the difference between caring for and caretaking, but they also help us separate quantity from quality. By setting limits, Terry recognized that if his father died, it would be after a compassionate exchange of time, energy, respect, and love, not a resentful one.

Here are a few more examples of less dramatic solutions to establishing limits:

- I'll only be able to go one more week.
- I'll explain this two more times.
- I can talk about this for thirty minutes.
- I'll give my boss one month to respond to my request.

5
Recapping: boundaries and limits

5

So when you are listening to somebody, completely, attentively, then you are listening not only to the words, but also to the feeling of what is being conveyed, to the whole of it, not part of it. —Jiddu Krishnamurti

Let's recap. The emotionally intelligent adult can easily set boundaries and limits that, depending on the individual situations and people, can be pulled in, extended, or shifted based on choice, new information, or more experience. Our boundaries and limits should be clear to us and to those we live with, love, or work with. Good boundaries and limits help protect us without isolating people or pushing them away. They keep us at a safe distance so that we don't have to accept anyone's rageful, shaming, abusive, or demeaning words, actions, or behaviors.

Good boundaries and limits actually increase intimacy, clarity, and communication and decrease vulnerability because you can say "no" when you need to. You can also say "yes" when you want to. You know where you stand, and this lets others know more about you. It enhances other people's feelings of safety and trust because they can rely on you when you say, "No more," "Enough," "Stop," or, "It's okay, you can come closer." When we stay true to ourselves and don't compromise our boundaries and limits no matter what someone may think, everyone involved wins in the long run of the relationship. But if we do compromise, we can end up becoming very codependent, which seriously undermines any of our efforts to become more emotionally intelligent people.

6

Discovering how codependency still affects your life after all these years

6

Teach us to care and not to care
Teach us to sit still.
—T. S. Eliot, "Ash Wednesday"

Codependency has become a familiar term these days. You hear it mentioned often in sitcoms. But the concept is still very misunderstood and remains one of the leading causes of divorce, misunderstandings, pain, and relationship problems at home and work.

What codependency really is

So what is codependency anyway? Codependency is an immersion in, and preoccupation with, everybody's business but your own. It is making sure everyone else's needs are taken care of while neglecting your own needs. Picture this scene at a holiday gathering. Mother is waiting on everyone hand and foot: "Does everyone have enough turkey?" "Who needs cranberry sauce?" "Let me get you some bread." She runs herself into the ground. Someone finally says, "Mother, sit down and eat. Everything is fine." Mom looks tired but still eager to please. "I'll sit down after everyone is through." "I'll grab something while I'm cleaning up the table and in between washing dishes, dear." "You go ahead and enjoy yourself, I'll eat next year." Alright, it isn't that funny—but isn't it also a little too true?

Codependency is an unfair, uneven exchange of energy. The codependent gives and gives and gets little, if anything, in return. The codependent enters a room feeling good, happy, and full of energy only to see someone sad, tired, and lonely. The classic codependent leaves feeling sad, tired, and lonely but satisfied that the other person feels much better than before they spoke together.

Codependency is the way people numb their own feelings. Okay, you're not addicted to alcohol, drugs, work, rage, sex, or gambling. But codependency will numb a person's feelings of sadness, anger, hurt, fear, or loneliness as well as any traditional medications can. By focusing on someone else's feelings, you don't have to deal with your own. Codependency is in many ways the disease of selfishness. When you micromanage another person's life, then you don't notice that your own life has become completely unmanageable. You end up looking like the healthy, more compassionate, intelligent, spiritual one—at least on the surface—and yet you can get just as addicted to this behavior as the heroin addict is to heroin.

Codependents are forever relying on external sources to make and keep them happy. If they have enough money, they're happy; if they don't, they're unable to be calm and at peace. If their children are happy, then they are happy. If their wives or husbands are doing well, then they feel they are doing well. If momma is happy or daddy is happy, then everyone in the family is temporarily comfortable and secure.

There is little or no ability in codependents to internally create peace of mind, serenity, self-esteem, and self-worth as they focus on others and, in the process, look damn good but are really burnt out.

The process of increasing emotional intelligence entails a great deal of new thinking, behaviors, and actions which go against society's injunction to appear selfless. Ironically, it is the codependent who is one of the most selfish among us.

7
Practicing a four-step model of grief work that increases emotional intelligence

7

*Grief is a normal and natural response to loss. It is
originally an unlearned feeling process. Keeping grief inside
increases your pain. —Anne Grant*

Grieving

Let's be clear. When a man, woman, or child is crying, it
is because the hurt has already occurred, and crying or
grieving is the healing of the hurt.

Many men and women fear sadness and grief because
they are afraid if they succumb to their sorrows, then the
black dog—depression—will devour their minds and souls.
Part of why this fear exists in so many is that we have confused grief with self-pity, which, if participated in long
enough, will turn into depression and depress the people

around us, eventually leaving us alone in a dimly lit place with only a glass of beer, playing to many "somebody-done-somebody-wrong" songs on the jukebox in our minds or in the beer joint.

Over the years I have been asked many times, "How do you start grieving, and what does it look like, sound like, and feel like?" Grieving is different for everyone, but here are a few things that are generally true for most.

Step A:

A person must become conscious of the necessity to grieve all their losses of any kind, no matter how big or small and no matter what anybody tells you or thinks. A person has to mourn not only the loss of things, people, places, pets, stages, transitions, and changes, but also everything they wanted but never got. Not having is a loss to be mourned, as was the case with James.

James is a data entry processor who told me how his mother married for the second time and had a child with his stepfather. She then devoted all her attention, support, and nurturing towards his half-brother. "She always took his side," he went on to say. "Even on her deathbed, she wanted him there and not me. She even refused to tell me anything about my real father."

We must also completely reject the toxic teachings that have become worn-out clichés when it comes to genuine grief work: *It's just water under the bridge; Let sleeping dogs lie; No use in crying over spilt milk; Get over it; Get back in the saddle; Pull yourself up by the bootstraps; Keep a stiff upper lip;* or *The past is dead and gone.* William Faulkner, the great Southern writer, said, "The past isn't dead, it's not even the past."

Step B:

You must develop a support network of people who will stand by you while you are grieving. These are friends, family, a therapist, God or another higher power, a sponsor, or all of the above—the more, the better. These people will not hurry you, shame you, or talk you out of your grief. Rather, they'll let you know, "We're here and we know grieving can be scary; that's why you shouldn't do it alone." In other words, use your community to hold your hand while you walk through what can feel like the "valley of the shadow of death."

One of the main reasons we put off grieving is that we have been told not to show our feelings and thus believe grieving should be a solitary act if an act at all. Grieving was never meant to be done entirely alone.

There is a tribe in the Polynesian islands that provides the best example of how grieving is a community job. When someone in the immediate family dies, it is everyone's job in that family to mourn and grieve the loss for a full year. During that year, tribe members take care of the children, the garden, the home, the cooking, and the cleaning for the grievers. At the end of the year, the grief cycle is completed because that was their sole—and soul—focus, and the family then resumes the business of life.

Step C:

Create a grief ritual. For example, it may be necessary to set aside time each day or once a week or whatever is appropriate for you. For instance, you may get up thirty minutes early before going to work and take your ex's picture out, light some candles or put on yours and her favorite music, and look at the photograph and tell her how you feel and what you loved and hated about your togetherness, and then weep, wail, get angry, or do whatever, then get up and take a shower and go to work.

Roger, an energetic man in his late sixties, once helped organize one of my workshops in South Dakota several years ago. He had been a professor of English at the university there for thirty-five years and had recently retired. As we were driving to the campus auditorium where I was to speak, he pointed to a building and said, "See the last window on the corner of the fourth floor? That was my office for thirty-five years." I said, "I bet there is a lot of you still in that room after all those years." He then said something I'll never forget: "Not an ounce." I was taken aback to say the least. "How is that possible after all those years?"

"I listened to your tape on grieving, and I did what you suggested because I didn't want any of me floating around in that building when I left. I wanted closure, so when I started my new life, I had completely said good-bye to my old one and honored it in the best possible way I could. Every Friday for a whole year I would sometimes have my students in for little get-togethers. Other times I had my faculty friends over for drinks. Some Fridays I just sat alone in my office and recalled some of my fondest memories, but every Friday I did something to say good-bye to my office, my profession, my students, and my friends, and at the end of that year, I was just full of gratitude for the time spent there."

Most people do not participate in ritual grief work like Roger. Instead, what most do—if they do anything at all—is what I call hit-or-miss grieving. They will start and stop and catch as catch can. They will do a lot for a day or two or a week and convince themselves they are finished; or some idiot—sometimes their own therapist or sponsor—tells them they "should be done" and move on. Or they might go to a grief workshop and do a whole weekend's worth. I don't think your twenty-year marriage or your one-year relationship can be grieved in a weekend, and the only person who will know when you are done is you. Remember, a ritual is something you do over and over again until it is no longer necessary. Some last for weeks, months, years, or lifetimes. Most grief rituals usually take six months to a year.

Step D:

I've found it to be important to have a ceremony at the end of the grieving process. This can be done by, say, inviting your friends who stood by you to someplace special—your favorite restaurant or park—and thanking them for the support they gave. This will let them and you see that you navigated the treacherous waters that flowed in your body's ocean of grief. Do you remember Alice in Wonderland? Well, the only way she could get through the huge locked door was to cry and cry, and pretty soon she raised herself on her own river of tears and floated right through the keyhole to the other side of the door—and the other side of her life.

How will you know it is time to do the ceremony? Because you will be in a place to celebrate the time spent between you and the person or thing you've been grieving. You'll be able to praise your ex and yourself for all the gifts you gave each other and all the lessons you learned; you will focus on the good parts of your old job. The pleasant memories of your parents are likely to surface, and even the good things you learned from your ex magically appear. Like Roger, you will find yourself feeling gratitude for the time spent at your job. You will be expressing gratitude for the time you spent in whatever relationship it was that is now over, and there will be no residual grief, anger, or resentment. Instead, you will bless the person, place, or situation. These are all signs that you have successfully come through this time of loss or change. However, if you are still angry, sitting in some bar drinking and telling the bartender or a stranger that the divorce papers were finally signed and now you are "rid of the bitch," or how much you hated all those years at your job, you're not done—you probably need to go back to step A.

I have also been asked many times, "When one begins the grieving process, how long does it take?" Some people may take a month to say good-bye gracefully, and someone else may be grieving a similar thing but could take a year or more. Time is a key element of grief work.

At a workshop on grief, a man asked me, "What do you do if you are already in a relationship, but you didn't make time to grieve the last one? Won't this upset my partner, to see me grieving another woman?" First of all, know that emotionally intelligent partners tend to know whether memories, love, or sadness are still floating around in someone's psyche or body. A healthy partner will give their partner time and will support their loved one to get the past out of their body, dreams, nightmares, and soul for the very reason mentioned above: it will make room in their heart for the present person they love and cherish.

8
Understanding boundaries, limits, and grief work through an adult fairy tale

8

Some day you will be old enough to start reading
fairy tales again. —C. S. Lewis

Most people think fairy tales are only for children. If we look more closely, we will find fairy tales, fables, and stories from quite a few cultures that were written for or told to adolescents, young adults, middle-aged folks, and even elders. The one I am about to tell you is about many things but most importantly it is about the need to grieve the past so that the present and future can be fully inhabited and celebrated.

Once upon a time, there was this King and Queen who wanted a child more than anything. They couldn't have one no matter how many fertility clinics they went to. So the Queen heard about this Wise Old Woman who lived in the woods who knew about such problems, and so she went to see her. The Woman told the Queen she could help her conceive if she would carefully follow her instructions. "Take a bath and throw the water under your bed. In the morning there will be two flowers—a red one and a white one. Eat the white one and not the red one, and you will give birth in nine months." The Queen did what she said except—you guessed it—just like all greedy men and women would, she thought, If one flower is good, then two have to be twice as good, so she ate both flowers. Nine months later they called for a Midwife to deliver the baby. During labor the Queen gave birth first to a little black snake. The Midwife knew no one likes snakes, so she threw it out the window without showing it to the Queen.

Question: What part of yourself was thrown out? That part must be grieved.

Then came the second baby, which was beautiful, and would grow up to be the golden boy Prince who made mom and dad very happy. He made straight A's, was captain of the football team, and graduated from Kingdom College summa cum laude. Now it was time for him to get married. The King told the Prince to go to the neighboring kingdom and court the Princess and marry her.

The Prince rode over one day, and in the middle of the road stood this huge, ugly snake. "Where the hell do you think you are going?" he hissed at the Prince.

"I'm going to date a Princess and marry her," he replied.

"Oh, no you're not. The Older Brother has to marry first according to our customs. No bride for you until I get a bride for me."

Well, all this confused the Prince. He didn't know he had a brother. What would his life have been like if he'd had a brother looking out for him? (If you are an only child, you may know this feeling all too well.) The Prince went back and told the King about this, and the King said it must be a mistake and to go again. But the same thing happened about three times. The snake blocked his way and demanded that he be married first. Finally, the King had had enough and wanted to get to the bottom of this, so he spoke to the Queen about this snake, and she didn't have a clue as to whom it could be. So finally he called in the Midwife, and she confessed. The King then decided to find this ugly snake a bride not blessed with cover-girl beauty and get him married so his golden-haired son could get married and inherit the kingdom. So he looked all around his kingdom for a suitable bride. He put an ad in the classifieds saying, "Single, slithery snake seeking lifelong partner, not very good table manners, and too many other bad habits to mention." You'd be surprised how many takers there were. Emotionally unintelligent women answered in droves. Some women love snakes, it seems, especially the tall, dark, and handsome ones, with lots of intensity and potential.

A beautiful bride was selected, and they had a wedding. But on the wedding night, the snake ate his bride. The King ran another ad and a second responded. And there was a wedding, and again, the snake ate his bride that night. And so it went with the third, fourth, and fifth. The women of the kingdom were hearing about the snake's taste in women, so they were getting a little harder to find.

However, there was a woodcutter's daughter, who was extremely in touch with her own emotions, and decided to go for it. Unlike her predecessors, she went to find the Wise Old Woman in the woods—the same one who helped the Queen get pregnant—and asked her for advice. She gladly gave it but insisted that unlike the Queen, she must follow her instructions to the letter or she could also become snake food. The Wise Old Woman told her to take her time and not rush into anything. You may recall the times you didn't listen to the wiser part of you saying, "This time go slow." That is a common mistake that often leads to loss, which will then require some grief work. The old woman told her to make seven beautiful wedding blouses and wear them on her wedding night, and to take a bucket of sweet milk and a steel brush with her to the bedroom. So she took about a year making these blouses. Waiting makes impatient snakes hungry. Finally, on the wedding night, the snake closed the door and was ready to have some wife food. But first he wanted a little pre-dinner show, so he said, "Take off your blouse."

"I'll take off my blouse if you will take off one of your skins," she replied.

"Do what? You've got to be kidding. That would hurt like

hell. Besides, no one has ever asked me to do this before." But, fueled by his hidden desire for real love, he began taking off his skin, and you should have heard the shrieks, cries, and yelling. You know it hurts to shed a skin. It also hurts to learn how to love. This snake had a lot to learn about how poorly he had loved in the past.

The woodcutter's daughter took off the blouse only to reveal another one under it. The snake looked perplexed and was beginning to get a little frustrated.

"Take off the blouse," He growled.

"I'll take off my blouse if you will take off your skin."

"I can't believe you're asking me to do all this stuff. No other woman I've eaten—I mean, loved—has ever asked me to do this before. What do you want from me? Emotional intelligence, honesty, availability? What next? I suppose you want me to open up and tell you what I really feel?"

So once again, you should have heard the moaning and groaning of the snake shedding another layer of skin. The woman removed a blouse only to reveal another one. Well, the snake was getting pretty irritated, to say the least, and was beginning to get the picture that this woman was not going to be as easy as the other brides, and that she knew how to take care of herself and ask for what she wanted and wouldn't settle for anything less than what she deserved. How many times have we all settled for less than we truly wanted or even deserved? Well, to make an already long story short, this went on for seven times until finally there was nothing left of the snake except a little puddle of a former self lying on the floor. That's what grieving and learning to really love will do to a snake (or an emotionally immature man): reduce him to nothing and show him he knows nothing about mature relationships. The bride took her bucket of sweet milk out from under the bed and dipped her steel brush into it and scrubbed what remained of the snake for about an hour or so. She would love him well. She prepared herself to love him well, and in so doing, prepared herself to be well-loved. The next morning the wedding chamber doors opened, and out stepped a beautiful, stunning Prince with his smart, respected bride, and they got the family together and had a great feast and lived happily ever after.

The snake didn't know the previous women he married and then ate. Carl Jung referred to these women as the "false brides." The "true bride" is the maiden with the seven blouses who took her time, took care of herself, had great boundaries, knew her limits, and demanded that the snake mourn his losses so that he would truly know himself and her. The snake thought that he was simply a giant snake, but there was so much more to him, and while the bride-to-be knew this, she was prudent and patient enough with him so that he found out just who his true self really was—a man who had experienced many losses in his life but had never been told or supported to grieve and mourn those losses, changes, and transitions that we all experience in our adult lives.

9
Experiencing and expressing anger appropriately

9

Holding on to anger is like grasping a hot coal with the intent of throwing it at someone else; you are the one who gets burned. —Buddha

"Thinking" we are expressing our anger

Many people have been taught, especially since the sixties, that we are not supposed to "hold in" our feelings of anger and that we are to "confront," "encounter," or have someone "call us on our stuff." This was a movement in the right direction, but most people do not feel safe with any of these bold terms of expression.

Here are some unhealthy ways anger is expressed, in part because no one showed us how to express anger appropriately.

Manipulating

Manipulating people is by far one of the more common ways anger leaks out, usually unknowingly. When we are angry, we manipulate those around us, giving us a momentary sense of power—the opposite of feeling angry, which usually leaves us feeling powerless. Jim was angry, to say the least, at his wife, who he felt did not appreciate the way he worked all the time to "keep her in the style which she had grown accustomed to as a child." So, he would attend social functions by himself even though both had been invited. He would convince her that she wouldn't enjoy the place or the people he associated with, and that she would be much happier staying at home. Jim would then drink too much and flirt with every woman there.

Controlling

Control is the kissing cousin of manipulation. Angry people are usually very controlling people. They try to control people, places, and things. They are like giant chess players moving the pawns around the board, partly because they are bored, but mostly because they're angry and just do not know it. Sometimes the moves they make are very subtle. We had a housekeeper who felt she should be doing more in this world with her life and was really too smart to clean toilets, so she was angry—not at my wife and me, per se, but at the circumstances of her life. She would rearrange everything on our desks and counters and in our closets and cabinets, and she would end up hiding things that we would spend hours looking for. Jackie's mother always had to drive when she was in the car, and if someone else said they wanted to, then she would change her mind last-minute about going unless they agreed to let her pilot the car. Jason refused to let his wife pay the bills, saying to her that it is "a man's job." Robin insisted her son of seven years to play soccer so he could "learn discipline," even though he didn't want to play. She kept telling him that someday he would thank her. Robert "gave" his wife an allowance each week as a way to keep her from spending their money on cocaine. He checked her odometer in her car each evening to see whether she used more than her allotted miles to go to the grocery store or pick up the children from school. When asked about this, he said he was just "helping" his wife not use.

Sabotaging

Sabotage is another cousin to manipulation and control. Rodney's mother abandoned him when he was ten years old. She ran off with the minister of her church, and he didn't hear from her again until he was twenty-eight years old. He was angry at her for leaving him with his alcoholic father, who was never there for him emotionally. In every relationship he got into, Rodney undermined his success and expressed his anger at women inappropriately by sabotaging all hopes of having a healthy relationship. Just when the relationship was beginning to go deeper, he would withdraw from her emotionally, shut down, and the next thing, become involved with another woman before he ran off the current one.

Joking

Telling really off-color, demeaning jokes is another form of anger leaking out of our overpressurized boilers. People who tell jokes about people of color and gay people are really just pissed off about something. Many of you reading this right now may be ready to close the book, thinking I'm trying to be politically correct or that I'm perhaps a little anal retentive. Before you stop reading, put yourself in these people's places and think how you would feel if you were called some of the demeaning names. Probably angry. One of the ways people justify their verbal punches in "putting people down" is to throw out the outworn phrase, "I'm just joking." Any time you have to add that phrase, it probably isn't a joke.

Almost everyone has had a "friend" who puts them down. Bill had a wife who would put him down in public and then right after doing so would always add, "I'm just kidding. He knows I love him." Here in the South we have the ability to say anything nasty we want to about someone as long as we add at the end of it, "Bless his heart." "Sherry is the worst mother in the world—she doesn't bathe that child of hers, she drinks all day long, and ain't got the sense God gave a billy goat—bless her heart."

Shaming

Shaming folks is done so frequently we hardly even notice it, though we feel it engulfing our bodies like the toxic ooze it really is. Jim's father would try to show him how to build things. When Jim wouldn't catch on fast enough, his father would say, "You can't be my son. We must have gotten the wrong baby at the hospital. My son would be able to fix or build anything, just like I do."

"What do you know? You were raised in the sticks," Tom's wife said when she was angry.

"Your feet are too big for your little body," Beth Ann often heard from her father.

"Shame on you," Lisa's mother often told her.

Blaming

Blaming is employed when folks are angry. They use statements like: "It's all your fault." "Look at what you've done now."

"We wouldn't be in this mess now if you had gotten that job in New York," Robin told her husband in my consulting room as they fought about finances. Jessie said to her husband George as she was packing up to leave him, "If you had only gone with me to counseling like I asked you to years ago, we wouldn't be getting a divorce now."

Demeaning

"Look at how your mother raised you," said Robert to his daughter about his ex-wife.

"Can't you tell time? When the big hand is on twelve and the little hand is on twelve, that's when we meet for lunch," I sarcastically said to a girlfriend decades ago while confronting her about constantly being late for engagements.

Demoralizing

Demoralizing comes in different disguises. "Your brother is the one with the brains in this family." "I don't think you're ever going to understand me." "Men are pigs—bless their hearts."

Criticizing

Criticism is so common that most of us think it's actually okay to receive or give it, whether it's asked for or not.

In my book *Facing The Fire: Experiencing and Expressing Anger Appropriately,* I have a chapter called "Saying No to Criticism," in which I discuss this issue. Most folks know way down deep in their guts that unsolicited criticism, even the kind that "is for your own good" or given "because I love you," stings like a thousand bees. As we pull the stingers out, those folks wonder what is wrong with us for taking it so badly; after all, we were just given "constructive criticism."

Unless you ask someone to give you their opinion, feedback, input, or—yes—criticism, it's probably only going to make you angry. But if you open the door and ask, you will almost always thank them for their honest comments. For example, before I got ready to send this book to my publisher, I asked a half-dozen people to tear it apart and tell me what didn't work. But after it is edited, printed, released, and received, I don't want to hear negative things about my paper-and-ink child or what you think "I should have done" to make it better. This sounds a little like the next thing people do when they are expressing their anger.

Preaching

Preaching "the gospel according to you" is a familiar approach to releasing anger, especially for Southerners who grew up always within earshot of a pulpit and an angry preacher pounding out his rage to those on the pews who believe he is talking straight to them while damning everyone to an eternity of fire and brimstone. Or how about the rigid 12-step sponsor who says, "Only turn it over to your higher power " or "I know the right way" or "I'll be praying for you every day," which is usually more of a censure than a loving offer.

Teaching

You take a wannabe preacher and send them to college and give them a little knowledge and you have a teacher, who is slightly subtler in the way he or she plans to get their message across. These angry folks tend to read self-help and recovery books addictively, underlining or highlighting in obnoxious pink or yellow markers everything they read because they know it applies to you. Then, equally as subtle, they leave the book lying in the sink or on your pillow, open to the page that most clearly shows who is the real problem, all the while thinking they are just being helpful.

Judging

The judge is the angry man or woman who thinks they are telling you how they feel but are really just judging your actions, behaviors, motivations, character, and personality. In reality, judges are telling the listener more about you than they are about themselves. The really good judge also gets to play two other roles—jury and executioner. The judge gets to find them guilty beyond a shadow of a doubt and impose the sentence they see fitting to the crime.

Analyzing

"Now that I have analyzed you, delved deeply into your psyche and soul, and picked apart your life and your brain, I am ready to make my recommendation to the rest of your family and friends. Now don't get me wrong—I'm not angry with you, I'm just trying to figure you out. I've looked at your mother and studied carefully your father, and I think I am ready to write up my diagnosis and 'share' with you my prognosis."

Still unsure whether any of this applies? Listed below are a number of telltale signs that a person may be angry. All of the following are raging behaviors.

Rigidity

Rage takes the form of a rigid body; rigid thinkers fear flexibility because flexible people feel.

All-or-nothing attitude

"Either go and see a counselor, or we're through," said Joseph to his wife. He felt he knew the "only way for her to be helped" was to do what he said—the old "my-way-or-the-highway" form of rage.

Black-and-white thinking

"You're wrong and I'm right." "All Muslims are terrorists." "Dad was a mean drunk, Mother was a saint." An extreme point of view can be a form of rage.

Verbal threats

"If you don't go into therapy, I'm leaving you." "If you leave now I won't be here when you return." "Go to bed and get to sleep before I come in there—and you don't want me to come in there." "Stop crying or I'll give you something to cry about."

Word games

"You call me critical, but I'm just concerned about your happiness." "I didn't say that exactly . . ."

We've all heard these things so often. We've seen these behaviors displayed in some way by our loved ones, and we've done them, too—so often that we've come to think this is just the way life is.

Exercise

On a scale of 1 to 5 (1 = never), circle the number to determine the extent to which you or your partner tend to employ these forms of anger:

Shaming	1	2	3	4	5
Blaming	1	2	3	4	5
Criticizing	1	2	3	4	5
Preaching	1	2	3	4	5
Teaching, that is patronizing	1	2	3	4	5
Judging	1	2	3	4	5
Analyzing	1	2	3	4	5
Sarcasm	1	2	3	4	5
Put-downs	1	2	3	4	5
Jokes at other's expense	1	2	3	4	5
Sabotaging	1	2	3	4	5
Controlling	1	2	3	4	5
Manipulating	1	2	3	4	5
Lying	1	2	3	4	5
Gossiping	1	2	3	4	5
One-upsmanship	1	2	3	4	5

Now, look at the boxes where you checked 4s and 5s. You may need a little work in these areas.

10
Stopping confusing anger and rage

10

Anger is a killing thing: it kills the man who angers, for each rage leaves him less than he had been before—it takes something from him. —Louis L'Amour

Seeing the difference between rage and anger

Unfortunately, many of us—and I include myself—use certain words interchangeably just as if they mean the same thing. Many say self-pity when they mean grief. Others confuse sympathy and empathy. But the words "anger" and "rage" are constantly spoken in the same sentence by therapists, counselors, and the general public, educated and noneducated alike. They do not mean the same thing. Anger is a feeling that comes and goes and doesn't do any damage to the body or the soul. It is an emotion that moves in, through, and out of the body and can usually be expressed quickly. Rage, on the other hand, is not—I repeat—is not a feeling but an action or behavior that is used to numb our feelings and medicate our emotions temporarily. Rage is just as effective in numbing our feelings of sadness, fear, loneliness, and—yes—even anger, as any drug, narcotic, or stimulant, alcohol, food binging-and-purging, sex addiction, or workaholism. Rage is legal, plentiful, and readily available.

When I am shaming, blaming, or demeaning you, I am raging at you. I am not feeling anything. When I am demoralizing, criticizing, preaching at, teaching (in a patronizing manner), judging, or analyzing you, I am not telling you how I feel. I am not opening my inner emotional self to you. I am in my head, not feeling a thing, but subconsciously wanting you to feel terrible about what you said or did, didn't say or didn't do that scared me, hurt me, made me sad, or made me angry. Now the politically correct among my readers are saying to themselves, No one can make you feel anything. And perhaps you are right, but bear with me a few more moments.

Likewise, when I am interrogating you, intimidating you, distancing myself from you, or playing the "poor me," I am using behaviors and taking actions to make my feelings go away temporarily just as well as drinking alcohol or ingesting a drug will do.

So when my clients or workshop participants tell me their husbands, wives, or parents are very angry, what they really mean to say is that they are raging. For example, my ex-love's father was not an angry man—he was a man full of rage, behaved and acted like a man full of rage, and made many sexist, racist, and gay-bashing statements. When a mother beats her children with her hairbrush, she is not angry, she is outraged. She is acting, behaving, and not feeling, because if she were truly feeling her feelings, she would also feel in her body that she must not hit her children.

How to tell the difference between anger and rage

There are a number of ways to tell the difference between rage and anger:

- Rage takes a long time to express—hours, days, weeks, months, years, and lifetimes.
- Anger expressed appropriately takes minutes at most.
- Rage is never resolved in a short conversation.
- Anger is often resolved in a sentence or two, maybe even three or four.
- Rage consists of paragraphs, pages, volumes, and epics.
- With rage there is no relief when expressed.
- Anger expressed relaxes us and sometimes even the other person because they feel safer with us now that they know how we feel.
- Rage always equals distance, disaster, and, frequently, divorce.

- Appropriate anger equals closeness, order, and clearer communication.
- When men, women, or children rage, everyone feels tired and drained.
- When we express anger appropriately, we usually feel refreshed and rejuvenated.
- Rage tends to hurt everyone in the vicinity.
- Proportional anger tends to hurt no one.

Let me be a little repetitive here and say again: rage is an action or a behavior used to numb our feelings, and anger is just a feeling, not positive or negative, and generally hurts no one any more than expressing sadness or joy does.

Four styles of rage

There are four predominant styles of rage. All four are frequently used, but some people gravitate more to one or two styles.

The Interrogator

The Interrogator is the rager who has ways to make you talk.

"What time did I tell you to be home?" "Who were you with?" "How many times have we had this conversation?" "How much did you have to drink?" "What is your excuse?" "How many times have I told you?" "When are you going to visit?" "Why don't you ever call?"

The Interrogator employs a rapid series of questions to control, manipulate, shame, or judge, leaving everyone exhausted and willing to sign any confession just to get out of the cold cement room, with one dim lightbulb and a one-way mirror.

The Intimidator

The Intimidator is the man or woman who rages by getting big and loud and filling up the entire room with their gigantic roar. This is done to demean and demoralize those around them and make them feel small and silent.

The Intimidator curses loudly and throws objects off tables or desks. They often employ preaching, sarcasm, and put-downs.

Sometimes Intimidators fill up the room with silence so thick you can cut it with a knife. Everyone around them is whispering and walking on eggshells, hoping the intimidator won't snap. Intimidators believe might makes right, and they're always going to have the last word.

The "Poor Me"

The "Poor Me" rager is just as full of rage as the others but does not have enough energy to question or get large. The "Poor Me" feels like the victim in every situation and uses complaining, justifying, draining language to get their points across.

"Am I the only one who has to work around here? I clean up the house before going to work. I work all day long, fight the commute home, and when I get here the house is a mess again," say mothers (and sometimes fathers) everywhere. "You'd think after working all day and putting up with all that I have to put up with, I could come home and relax, but noooo!"

"I know I'm late for our lunch meeting," Jason said to his boss. "But just as I was getting ready to leave the office, this customer called, and he just kept talking and talking and I thought you were going to be mad at me for being late again. But what could I do? I had to talk to him. So boss, don't be angry at me for my tardiness. Let's go find the customer and chew him out."

You know you're a "Poor Me" if you are often asked in a sarcastic tone, "Would you like some cheese with your whine?"

The Distancer

The Distancer is the most prevalent style. The Distancer has one foot in and one foot out of every conflict, confrontation, and argument. They use one of the worst four-letter words in relationships, one that communicates nothing: *FINE.*

Cherie says she hears this word from her husband all the time before he walks out the door. The Distancer also uses the word "whatever" quite a bit. Both words basically say, "I'm out of here and I'm not going to tell you where I'm going or when I'll be back, and you can do whatever you want and I'll say it's fine, but really it isn't fine at all."

If you want to be a good Distancer, just put these two words together: *"Fine! Whatever!"*

The Distancer is emotionally unavailable, shut down, and numb. He is "here" only in body, but he is absent in every other sense.

11
Identifying the En-rager and the Out-rager

11

People who fly into a rage always make a bad landing.
—Will Rogers

Enraged or outraged?

To make a distinction between what we normally think of and label as rage—hitting, slapping, pinching, pushing, or road rage—I am referring to the above examples as "soft rage." I'm sure by now you see there is no such thing. All rage hurts everyone involved. Most people lean toward being enraged or outraged. Oddly enough, En-ragers tend to partner with or marry Out-ragers. Out-ragers try to get the En-rager to ratchet up their behavior, and En-ragers try (sometimes for a lifetime) to tone the Out-rager's behavior down. As one person noted at a seminar, "We call this *marriage.*"

En-ragers tend to hold everything in, sometimes for days or even decades. They bottle their emotions up and try to put a lid on every feeling that is uncomfortable. They tend to stew, seethe, and get stressed out. En-ragers often employ shame, criticism, and very harsh judgment of others, holding in anger and then projecting it onto others. En-ragers internalize their fears, which turns into rage.

Out-ragers, on the other hand, externalize their fears instead of facing them. Out-ragers tend to be active in their persecution of others who don't feel, think, believe, or behave like them. Out-ragers curse loudly, throw things, scream, and never lower their voices. It's hard to say which of the two rage types is more dangerous to relationships.

Whether you find yourself or someone you know in either or both categories, take heart. You are about to be introduced to information that can help dramatically reduce anger and rage by turning both the En-rager and Out-rager into people who talk, act, think, and feel like what indigenous cultures refer to as "human beings." This will significantly increase emotional safety and therefore emotional intelligence.

You Might Be An En-rager If You:	You Might Be An Out-rager If You:
Stew and obsess	Yell or scream
Self-medicate with drugs, alcohol, food, sex, etc.	Throw things

Can't let go   Slam doors
Keep resentments   Break things
Fixate   Curse

12
Recognizing emotional regression

12

Do not dwell in the past. —Buddha

Emotional regression

Emotional regression is the best-kept secret in modern psychology. There is virtually nothing written on the subject, and certainly very little that explains it and relates it to everyday life, especially as it impacts anger and rage. (See my book *The Anger Solution: The Proven Method for Achieving Calm and Developing Healthy, Long-Lasting Relationships.*) There are many ways to define emotional regression, and you are likely very familiar with the following phrases related to it because either you've employed them recently or someone has said them to you:

"I wish you'd grow up."

"You're acting like a big baby."

Perhaps less common—but still a good way to define emotional regression—is an unconscious return to our past. When we regress, we are hurled into our past faster than lightning. We say things or react the way we did when we were in our twenties, teens, or childhood years. This is not the same as consciously drawing from the past to solve a problem in the present by remembering how we solved a similar issue earlier. Rather, it is an unconscious, unintentional revisiting of deep feelings and reactions we felt at one time, and find ourselves reliving over and over.

13
Eliminating the triggers
for regression

13

Do not brood over your past mistakes and failures as this will only fill your mind with grief, regret, and depression. Do not repeat them in the future. —Sivananda

Preconditions for regression

There are five physical, psychological, and emotional states that, if avoided, will minimize the number of times and tendencies to regress, feel small like a child, or lose it (i.e., our adultness—the composed, balanced, and rational way of looking at or dealing with things). I often point out that these states are not only common but also a part of almost everyone's personal and professional lives. Many workplaces, like Google, spend time and energy reducing these preconditions, which is part of the reason they receive over four thousand applications per day for employment.

Exhaustion

Mental or physical exhaustion greatly increases one's time in the past. Extreme tiredness can make a grown man or woman yearn for their carefree college days or a perpetually extended beach vacation. Exhaustion can take us out of the prefrontal, rational neocortex thought process, sending us to a preverbal state of either the reptilian brain or of an animal that curls up and takes a long winter's nap.

Exhaustion makes us more susceptible to verbal, emotional, or physical abuse from bosses, parents, our children, or authority figures. It makes our skin paper-thin, and we tend to lose our ability to say things like, "No," "No more," "Enough," or "Stop." We lack the necessary energy to take care of ourselves, so we are more likely to engage in codependent relationships, hoping to be rescued or saved for our ultimate well-being.

When we're tired, we can't think about the big picture. We exchange things that are good for us for short-term, temporary fixes, settling for much less than we want or deserve in personal or professional situations and even relationships. We have a "short fuse"; we're grouchy, irritable, impatient, and impractical. We say and do things we may regret for years to come. We rage at the too-slow lady in front of us at the store checkout line and swear at the DMV.

Hunger

When a person has gone too long without food—there's that word again, too—the brain loses oxygen and blood flow.

That, in turn, leads to a lack of self-soothing chemicals like serotonin, neoepinephrine, and oxytocin. Extreme hunger makes us lose our patience, poise, and practicality. Hunger takes us back to infancy as quickly as anything can. Once our blood sugar is significantly altered, we yell at spouses when supper is not served on time, much like we did in the crib when nourishment was slow in coming. Adults who are very hungry watch the second hand on their watches to see whether the waitress indeed comes to the table in "a minute" after seating us. We may swear at the waitstaff as if they were slaves instead of servers.

Stress

Stress increases distress. When people are distressed, they get tense. Tension leads to contraction of body, mind, and soul. Contraction creates rigidity and narrowness of mind and heart. When people are stressed and in distress, you can give them suggestions, advice, feedback, counseling, books to read, and counselors to see—and none of it is taken in. All roll right off the stressed, regressed person like water off a duck's back, and they often even feel offended and let you know it in no uncertain terms by raging.

Not much that comes out of the mouth of stressed, distressed individuals makes much sense. It usually lacks coherency and continuity; conversations are convoluted and confusing at best.

Now for the bad news—as if the above wasn't bad enough—when we hear the word "stress," we immediately think, Welcome to the American workplace, where stress has become the norm. Americans are working harder and longer and with less vacation time than ever. The cost of living rises while jobs are scarce and salaries decline. Work is outsourced to other countries. The average American worker is scared, exhausted, disconnected, and regressed.

The other negative quote we hear in our heads about stress is Welcome to the average American home. Both parents are working, trying to make ends meet. Children have less supervision and interaction with parents, particularly fathers. Studies show that on average, fathers spend less than two hours per week with their children. In much of the Western world, divorce occurs in one out of two marriages; thus, more and more children are being raised in one-parent homes. When all of these factors come together, you have stress, distress, more and more regression, and more and more unabated rage.

Illness

Minor or major illness may turn a grown man or woman into a big baby who wants to curl up and be fed and read to. Don't get me wrong, there's not a thing wrong with this. It's just that when illness strikes, maturity, rationality, reasonability, sound judgment, and sound decision-making often go right out the door of the sick room. Instead of requesting nurturing and comfort, some of us actually go into work anyway or refuse to go see the doctor. We want to deny our condition or have someone come take care of us, but we don't ask.

Pressure

Pressure to perform, pressure to please, pressure to achieve, pressure to be or not to be. Although that may be the perennial question, the answer is that pressure causes regression. Remove the pressure, and you'll no longer feel like you are an awkward adolescent or a stumbling toddler who can barely walk—let alone speak coherent, intelligent sentences.

Pressure leaves adults exhausted. Pressure makes us forget to eat or rest as we wrestle with real or imaginary deadlines. Enough pressure exerted long enough on coal turns it into a diamond, but too much pressure on people turns them into regressed, raging lumps of coal, too exhausted to move.

14
Seeing the signals that you or someone else is regressing

14

*The taste for worst-case scenarios reflects the need to master
fear of what is felt to be uncontrollable. —Susan Sontag*

Signs of regression

Remember, different things cause people to regress differently and in different ways, but there are a few almost universal signs and signals that we are heading into our past. These signals apply to both the one triggering the regression and the one who is regressing.

Story Time

You can never cure regression, but you can know the signs that you are beginning to regress. Once these are recognized, you can catch yourself before descending into the past or becoming the incredible shrinking man or woman. One of the more obvious signs is Story Time.

Here's an example: James is a boss who is experiencing regression. On Friday afternoon, he says to his employee Alex, "I want to see you in my office first thing Monday morning." What does Alex do? If statements like James's trigger an emotional memory, like the one Alex has of his mother saying something such as "Wait until your father gets home," or a teacher's threat like "The principal is out today but he will deal with you Wednesday," Alex will begin Story Time. All weekend long he will make up stories about what James wants to talk about. Perhaps it was the fax paper he took home? No, wait. It was the personal charges made on the corporate card, or maybe it's worse—termination. With each worst-case story, Alex gets angrier and angrier and then finally settles into rage. No one in the history of employment has ever made up the story, "Hey, I bet he wants to talk about that raise I so readily deserve." When Alex has exhausted all possible stories and gets to James's office, he is exhausted and feeling about five inches tall.

This chart breaks it down:

Regressed Boss	Employee – Regressed Reaction	Employee – Adult Response
Says, "I want to see you in my office first thing Monday morning," and nothing else.	*Thinks, I'm going to be fired! Spends all weekend obsessing and creating worst-case scenarios. Comes into work on Monday upset, stressed, and feeling five inches tall.*	*Thinks, Maybe this is about the Smith account, or maybe I'm going to get a raise. But since he didn't give me any more information, I'll just wait until Monday and I won't worry about it.*

When we regress, we almost always create worst-case stories. Interestingly, Story Time is a regressed attempt to self-soothe and calm our fears, but this attempt backfires, and the end result is more anxiety—not less—and deeper regression. Ironically, it is these same fictitious stories that increase fear, anger, rage, and regression because they appear in living color from that part of the brain that is illogical and irrational. These semi-paranoid parables can get quite extreme, ranging from the temporary belief that someone is plotting to get you to the idea that someone is conspiring to control or perhaps even annihilate you.

Cheri is a stay-at-home mother. Twice divorced, she has trouble trusting her current husband. Her first husband died in a car crash, and her second one cheated on her with another woman. While she has worked on her anger and grief, she doesn't quite trust that Thomas, who she says is a fine man, will not eventually leave her.

Thomas had to go to Chicago on a business trip. He told her he would be in his hotel no later than 10:00 and would call her no later than 10:30. Cheri waited by the phone like a teenager waiting for her first crush to call. Well, 10:30 came—no call; 10:35—still no call. Cheri has had a good deal of therapy, so she didn't regress until 10:40.

"I wanted to know where he was. I bounced between anger, rage, and fear like a tennis ball. I started thinking something bad had happened to him; perhaps a car accident or the plane went down. I couldn't stop the terrible pictures that flashed through my mind as I waited for him to call. I saw him lying helpless or maybe dead in some ditch somewhere or in an emergency room. I was panicking. Then all of a sudden, I pictured him with his secretary who went with him to that meeting, and I thought, That son-of-a-bitch better be dead in a ditch because if I catch him with his secretary, I am going to kill him! She was crying and laughing at the same time as she told me this story.

If no one in your life has ever wrecked their car, been taken to the emergency room, or cheated on you, then you would have said to yourself about a situation similar to Cheri's, I guess the plane was delayed, and I'm sure they are alright and will call in the morning. You would have turned out the light and slept like a baby—and by "like a baby" I mean you wouldn't have woken up every hour screaming and crying, wondering where your mommy was. No. You sleep like an adult who does not convince yourself of worst-case stories.

Child Time

A four-year-old says to her mom or dad, "When are we going to go see Grandma?" The look of excitement and expectation turns into desperation when the parent replies, "In two weeks." Two weeks is an eternity for a child. You may recall how summers lasted forever and Christmas never came.

A forty-year-old man goes to the doctor on Monday because of some condition that produces concern and anxiety. The doctor speeds in, checks him over, and on his way out says, "We'll have these tests back on Friday, so try not to worry." Monday to Friday feels how long? Like an eternity. It is almost exactly the same feeling or concept of time that children have, because the adult has regressed and is back in Child Time, which is full of worst-case stories.

When men and women regress, time gets weird. Regression leads to time being compressed or expanded to the point that it is dreamlike. Minutes feel like hours, hours feel like days, days seem like months and months, and months can be decades. But the good news is once you know this to be a sign of regression, you can catch it and bring time back to its normal feel, thus reducing anxiety and fear.

When we regress, time also contracts. If you are reading this newly in love or remember being newly in love, you may recall that time collapsed in on itself—the brand-new lovers have fallen in love. We don't say we have progressed or moved forward in love. No, we fall right back to our childhoods, leaving adult time and descending into that oceanic oneness we experienced in the womb, or at our mother's breast. When we fall, we begin conversations with our loved one at 8 p.m., only to come out of the ecstatic trance at 2 a.m. with one of us saying something like, "Can you believe what time it is? We have been talking for six hours. Where did the time go?"

Disproportional energy

I'm sure everyone reading this has either said or heard someone say to them, "Where is all of this coming from?" "This" being all of their excessive energy about the problem or issue being discussed. The disproportional amount of energy feels overwhelming for many and just plain scary for others.

Those on the receiving end often feel they are being flooded by the speaker's words of unfair accusations, insinuations, and criticism. This torrent of energy is usually not enthusiasm but judgment and shame. Therefore, the listener tends to feel pushed away or wants to run away. But most of all, the listener feels confused.

"Why is he talking to me this way?" Jill asked me one day during a consultation. "It's like he's talking to someone else and he doesn't even see me. Sometimes I think he's shouting at his first wife or his mother." I asked her how this made her feel. "I felt scared and angry. It pushed all my buttons, and I feel like a little girl back in my parents' house where I never felt seen either."

When the regressed person reacts disproportionally to

the event, problem, or person, it is always about their history. And no one likes to have another person's history dumped in their laps or into their hearts. We all have enough painful memories of our own. Now don't get me wrong, I'll be receptive if you're not regressing yourself to hear the other person's issues and if you both are in the present. But even when the listener is not regressed, he or she often will be after being hit with a barrage of hurtful words.

The physiology and brain chemistry of choicelessness

When men and women are regressed, one of the signs is they feel like they don't "have a choice." Choice is a function of the neocortex, or the new brain. Scientists tell us this portion of the human brain is roughly ten thousand years old. This new brain is capable of rational and logical thought processes. According to author Antonio Damasio in *The Feeling of What Happens,* the neocortex permits "fine perceptions, language, and high reason. It allows us to 'think' about our choices and reason out our options." The neocortex and the developed prefrontal lobes are basically inactive during the regressed state.

During regression, it is our reptilian brain, or "old brain," that is in charge. This section of the human brain is what we share with reptiles; it has been keeping humans safe for over one hundred thousand years. This brain is only capable of performing the most basic functions—eating, excreting, and procreating—and is limited when there is a threat to our physical or emotional survival, whether real or imagined. It tells us to do one of three things: fight, flight, or freeze.

When a painful, traumatic, hurtful, or unpleasant memory is triggered, we leave the neocortex, bypass the Limbic or mammal brain, and head straight to the reptilian brain. As Dr. Peter Levine states in his seminal work, *Waking the Tiger*, "For the reptile, conscious choice is not an option." He goes further to say, "The neocortex is not powerful enough to override the instinctual defense response to threat and danger."

The other option is to run away from the perceived threat to somewhere safe, like a cave—or the cave of our own minds, in this case—and hide until we are out of danger. If we can't do either, we go into freeze or suspended animation for the duration of the bad marriage, less-than-desired work situation, or other negative scenario. In other words, choices that can be seen by others regarding our particular regressive situation cannot be seen by us until we return to allowing the neocortex to dominate these decisions.

15
Working our way out of passivity: the hidden element that limits emotional intelligence

15

For the ordinary man is passive. . . . So far from endeavoring to influence the future, he simply lies down and lets things happen to him. —George Orwell

Passivity

Passivity has been one of the least studied, discussed, and explained aspects of human behavior. The fields of psychology, personal growth, and recovery have completely ignored it. Understanding passivity is an essential key to enhancing emotional intelligence, creating healthy relationships, increasing self-esteem, and healing the bodies, minds, and spirits of individuals who are hurting or hurting others.

Passivity is a compulsion or learned tendency to live at half-speed, which ultimately leaves people feeling their glass is half empty, and thus they halfheartedly commit to projects, plans, and goals. Passive people are half in and half out of relationships. The passive person is more attached to not having what they think they want or desire, even though they protest loudly that this is not so.

A client of mine, James, is forty and a very successful real estate agent who earns a high six-figure income. During a session he said, "I work all the time on my marriage. I'm in therapy, I read books, and I regularly attend self-help workshops. No one can say I'm passive." When asked about his marriage he quickly replied, "I want more physical contact, more touching, and yes, more sex, but I get hardly any at all."

James wants his wife, Brenda, to be more affectionate, yet he indulges in a whole host of behaviors that guarantees he'll get just the opposite of what he thinks and says he really wants.

I asked him to give me an example of his efforts to get affection from his wife, so I could see and show him his passivity and addiction to not having what he says he wants.

James said, "I go into the living room all the time, and Brenda is on the couch watching television for hours on end. I say something like, 'Can't you turn that thing off for a little while? There's nothing intelligent or worth watching on TV. I don't know why you watch these silly shows.' But she never agrees and I end up storming out of the room frustrated as usual."

I jokingly said, "How's that working for you?" Then I offered a suggestion. "Try sitting on the living room couch next to her, gently lifting her legs, and placing them on your lap while you massage her feet, instead of shaming, criticizing, demeaning, and judging her. Then simply ask her what's on that you two can watch together."

He looked at me like I was speaking in a foreign tongue; in a way it was an unfamiliar language because it was the language of compassion and assertiveness. James looked a little dumbfounded before saying, "No, I have never even thought of it. It sounds so simple. I can see me doing that but I never would have thought to do so. I wonder why?" he said very seriously.

It was because of his passivity and his fears of rejection, abandonment, and intimacy.

By the way, he tried my suggestion the very next week. "We got up off the couch ten minutes after doing what you suggested. She looked at me and said, 'Who are you?' Before I could answer she laughed and said, 'Never mind, I like this,' and we got up and got in bed and made love for the first time in a year."

This same man devoted an exorbitant amount of time to reading about relationships and marital counseling. He said he worked all the time on his marriage. But in reality, he thought his wife had the problem and not him.

Passivity is difficult to identify because one of the greatest tricks a passive person plays on themselves goes something like this: "Look how hard I work. I work eighty hours a week and am the CEO of a large company. How can anyone label me as passive?" or "Look how much I work on myself.

I go to five 12-step meetings a week and see my therapist regularly; how can I be passive?" "Can't you see I'm suffering? Isn't that proof that I'm not attached to passivity?"

One of the main symptoms of passivity is being out of balance in our personal and professional lives. The passive person's creed is, "I'm bored," or "I'm feeling overwhelmed," and they think the world acts on them and moves them rather than being actors and movers.

It is important to note that passivity causes you to react rather than act, control rather than respond, manipulate rather than make, or self-destruct instead of create. The passivity I am discussing is not to be confused with passive-aggressive behaviors, timidity, shyness, apathy, or laziness. It is also not to be misconstrued as surrendering or letting go, "turning it over," or practicing passive resistance. All of these are very active processes that actually energize the ones doing so. The passivity being discussed here is more akin to giving up, feeling hopeless, feeling defeated, settling for, or feeling unsatisfied.

Movement past passivity

By working with your tendencies to be passive, you are taking the first critical steps to take your life to the next level, a level that is more emotionally rewarding and satisfying. Unfortunately, many people have developed a greater connection to loss and feeling less than; they settle for unfulfilling relationships or careers that never quite allow them to achieve their creative potentials. Surviving rather than thriving has become the state that many are not only used to but are also compelled to pursue. It is the nonengaging that lets life pass you by because you did not have the information and tools to take action to change things for the better. You do now. Passivity is a learned behavior, a reaction to life that can be unlearned.

Passivity is an offense of omission—not doing or saying what you need to, not responding, not accepting challenges, and refusing to take risks—rather than of commission, and that is one reason it has been overlooked by clinicians and writers.

Passivity compels people to wait in a state of suspended animation until something or someone outside themselves "rescues" them from their current circumstances. This knight in shining armor (whether a person, the world, society, or a supernatural being) is supposed to bring the passive person something they feel they have lost or had taken from them. That something could be hope, energy, love, trust, faith, the perfect job, an unconditional lover, the winning lottery numbers, or the good parent they never had, once had, or wished they had. It is a psychological, physical, emotional, and spiritual condition that plagues even the most educated and self-directed people, and therefore, the whole person must be addressed. Once it is, you can move from passivity to pursuing your life passions and your relationships.

16
Becoming a more compassionate person

16

The whole idea of compassion is based on a keen awareness of the interdependence of all these living beings, which are all part of one another, and all involved in one another.
—Thomas Merton

I, not you

When we become truly ready to address our passivity and commit ourselves to continue to increase our emotional intelligence, one of the first active steps we take is to see the absolute necessity in dropping one of the most button-pushing, passive words in the English language: you. The differences between "I need" and "You need to," "I hurt" and "You hurt me," "I feel" and "You made me feel," "I love you" and "Do you love me?" are enormous, and the latter examples only perpetuate conflict and miscommunication. Besides, there is something about this three-letter word "you" that puts almost everyone in a defensive posture, causing them to duck and run for cover. It instigates "I'm out of here" or other "Distancer" behavior.

"If only you would . . ." "Why don't you . . ." "You should . . ." "You ought to . . ." Even the word "you" by itself triggers many defensive responses.

Intimacy ends with "you" and begins with "I." The word "I" is active, compassionate, responsible, remorseful, mature, and nonthreatening. It enhances connection and reduces needless confrontations and conflicts. "I" becomes the actor, instigator, and mover. You act upon me; you must be the initiator and move me from one place to another. It is the I who must feel my own feelings and communicate them to those I love and care about.

The compassionately assertive person

Until one is well-versed in the usage of emotional literacy, the tendency is to swing from being aggressive and inappropriate to passive and inappropriate when trying to convey how you feel. The more we increase our EQ, the more we learn that we can become assertive but in a healthy and direct way so that no one will get their feelings hurt.

The less often we regress and rage, the more often we will treat ourselves and also those we care about with compassion and tenderness and yet still feel powerful.

One of the greatest pluses the emotionally intelligent person experiences is they will learn to actively give and receive love in a mature adult way, something the passive person cannot do. Those not enhancing their EQ will tend to do what they were taught, and that is to show people love and support the way they themselves would like to be shown love and support. Compassionate men and women will send those they love the kind of love they need. High-EQ people, instead of passively following the Golden Rule (Do unto others as you would have them do unto you), will follow the Platinum Rule of compassion: Do unto others the way they need to be done to. Those you love have probably been yearning to be loved in that way their whole lives.

17
Engaging in active loving

17

Action is the real measure of intelligence. —Napoleon Hill

Four ways to love

The passive person puts so many limits on their love by expressing this emotion in only one or two of the following ways. They may be very good romantic partners but not so good at being friends. A man or woman might be very involved with their community and even include their spouse in the process, but they do not share any spiritual or erotic love.

The active-loving, emotionally available person works diligently and with commitment to learn and then express the following four kinds of love:

1. *Eros* – Erotic love
2. *Agape* – Spiritual love
3. *Philios* – Friendship love
4. *Caritas* – Love of community

By blending these four kinds of love, you can create true intimacy, more harmony, and a much more balanced relationship.

18
Understanding that wanting and needing are two different things

18

Our necessities never equal our wants.
—Benjamin Franklin

Saying what you want and need

Emotional intelligence helps us distinguish between wanting and needing. Wanting is "best-case scenario" or "wishful thinking," or having a fantasy fulfilled about how we desire things or someone to be. Wanting is negotiable. We can compromise on our wants; we can exercise a certain give-and-take.

Needing is much more serious and essential. Needs are akin to things that we cannot do without—air, water, food, et cetera. Needs are non-negotiable. There is no room for compromise. Needs are kissing cousins to boundaries and limits.

The compassionately assertive, emotionally present person can tell the difference between what they want and what they need. This helps them not run from clashes and disagreements, which are a part of every relationship, because they have the resources to handle them appropriately. They are emotionally equipped to finish the four assertive statements regarding requests of others and themselves:

1. This is what I want: _____.
2. This is what I need: _____.
3. This is what I will not do to get my wants and needs met: _____.
4. This is what I will do to get my wants and needs met: _____.

Example:

Cheryl is an active woman in her thirties. She runs, cycles, and is an avid mountain climber. She wants her husband to join her in these activities, but he is not athletically inclined at all. She needs him to support her to continue these activities and his support to be for friends who can share her passions.

Cheryl will not pressure her husband to be more involved in these areas. She will not shame him for not doing so.

What she will do is to continue to leave the door open should he ever want to join her, and she will continue to share her delight in pursuing her vigorous paths.

19
Identifying and pursuing your passion

19

We must act out passion before we can feel it.
—Jean-Paul Sartre

Remembering who you wanted to be

No matter how much we work on ourselves by improving our emotional health and well-being, if we are not doing what we love, we will almost always feel out of sync with ourselves, other people, and the world in general. In other words, we can do all the therapy, read all the self-help books, attend support groups, and travel to workshops, and if we are still pursuing a living that does not fully engage our entire being, we will not feel like we are moving forward.

One of the sure signs that a person is enhancing their

EQ is that they will follow their passions. Once passive people start digging their way out of the passive pit, they start reconnecting to their true selves. I often refer to this reconnection as "remembering who you wanted to be." Most people remember a moment in their childhood, or much later in life, when they realized what their passion, purpose, or calling was. They knew right then what they should do with their lives and careers, but because they were operating from a passive point of view and from a lower emotional intelligence, they didn't seek that dream because of fear, hopelessness, or lack of energy. Being passive takes a lot of energy. Let's say you've always wanted to be a portrait painter, but you are afraid that if you pursue your dream, you'll become the proverbial starving artist—destitute and homeless. In reality, what happens is that even if you, a passive person, end up living in a mansion, you will become emotionally (if not financially) destitute because you didn't pursue your passion, making you angry, distant, or depressed, or causing you to disappear into the work you don't even enjoy.

20
Getting out of the triangle tangle

20

He's my friend that speaks well of me behind my back.
— Thomas Fuller

Triangulation

In the words of Rod Sterling, the narrator of the hugely popular television show *The Twilight Zone:* "You are traveling through another dimension, a dimension not only of sight and sound but of mind. . . . Next stop, the Twilight Zone," or perhaps the emotional Bermuda Triangle. Many a good man or woman has been emotionally lost here for decades. They just disappeared into this emotional netherworld where no one talks to anyone directly, where family secrets are shared but not with everyone, and where nothing is above board or out in the open.

Everyone has heard of a "love triangle," but there is also an emotional triangle. Triangulation is like emotional strangulation in the sense that you can't speak out the words you want to or need to, to someone directly. The more dysfunctional a home is, the more it is filled with these triangles, and the more we see them, hear them, participate in them, and perpetuate them in the present, the angrier we become. A triangle's main purpose is to get uncomfortable messages to others through others. It is a flawed attempt, and a very often failed attempt, to get answers via another person.

Steven's mother tells him about his sister. Steven talks to his sister about his father. His father talks to his sister about Steven, and so on. Steven said to me, "It's been this way for over five decades and I hate it, but I don't know how to break out of it, we've done it for so long."

These triangles, whether they are constructed at home or work, become "the tangled web we weave" because at a certain level, we are actually being deceptive through omission, depriving ourselves and others of the benefits adults can have by speaking directly to those we need to speak to.

The damage done by "going behind their backs," "going through the back door," or taking the "roundabout" way gets everyone involved a little or a lot angry and increases distrust.

Ted said, "I called my ex-wife to find out how my oldest son, Bill, is doing, and I asked her to ask him to call me."

"What kept you from calling him directly?" I asked.

"I feel that he dismissed me from his life years ago. He

told me he didn't want to have anything to do with an alcoholic father."

"When was that?" I asked.

"About twenty years ago when I was drinking."

"Are you still drinking?"

"Oh no, I've been clean and sober for five years. But every time I think about calling him, I hear those words of his in my ears like it was yesterday."

How do you demolish triangles? By making more straight lines. By going directly to the person, family, group, teacher, or boss and saying what you need to say or asking for what you need.

21
Separating versus isolating

21

Therefore keep in the midst of life. Do not isolate yourself. Be among men and things, and among troubles, and difficulties, and obstacles. —Henry Drummond

Separating equals coming together

Emotionally intelligent people engage in separation instead of isolation. By age two, children begin the process of separating from their parents. By age twelve, they are fully engaged in the process unless the parents did not experience healthy separation from their parents, in which case they will tend to cling to their child and limit their adolescent's ability to move away from them in a healthy manner. This limiting, hovering, or clinging creates the tendency for teens—and later, adults—to move more and more towards isolation when they need time to themselves instead of allowing themselves the space they need to renew and regenerate their energy to be with lovers, friends, children, or parents.

Emotionally healthy people can see that separation generates closeness and intimacy because men and women can detach and disconnect when tired, overwhelmed, drained, or exhausted by too much contact and stimulation. They pull away in a functional way and then return ready for more communication, commitment, and caring.

Isolation leaves everyone in the dark because no one knows when the person is coming back, or if they ever will come back, and this isolation may trigger unexposed, unexplored abandonment issues. Isolators close themselves off to intimacy, which can result in anything from feeling distant to getting divorced to becoming depressed.

There are many forms the isolator can take on, but the main one the emotionally challenged person tends to favor is "Distancer." This is the person who, during conflict or confrontation, tends to say things like, "Fine, I'm out of here" or "Whatever" before walking or running away to work, alcohol, drugs, affairs, or other mind-numbing, body-numbing, emotion-numbing behaviors.

22
Making an appropriate apology

22

A stiff apology is a second insult . . . The injured party does not want to be compensated because he has been wronged; he wants to be healed because he has been hurt.
—G. K. Chesterton

A healthy apology

So you or someone you love has had a little trouble with setting appropriate boundaries, identifying limits, expressing anger instead of rage, ceasing to regress, grieving your losses, and separating instead of enmeshing. Perhaps you (or they) did it all wrong. What can you do?

Many men and women have never heard or, for that matter, spoken an appropriate, emotionally healing apology. The emotionally challenged person may never apologize at worst, or they may say "I'm sorry" at best but proceed to explain why they shouldn't have to apologize at all.

"I'm sorry I'm late for our dinner date, but you have to understand just as I was getting ready to leave the office, I got a call from a very important client, and so I really had to take that call. I'm sure you understand."

In other words: "I'm really not sorry at all."

One client of mine years ago said he actually only said the words "I'm sorry" when someone had passed away or experienced an unfortunate calamity or crisis.

What does an appropriate apology sound like? "I want to apologize for being late for this dinner." After just about anyone hears something like this, the response is almost always, "Thank you," or "No problem," "I appreciate it," or "I accept your apology, let's eat." Ensure that your apologies are heartfelt and healthy as well, with no excuses.

23
Making amends and becoming emotionally mature

23

*If you have behaved badly, repent, make what amends
you can and address yourself to the task of behaving better
next time. —Aldous Huxley*

A clean amends

The emotionally mature person will often feel obligated
or motivated to make amends for something they have
done or said that requires an apology. In other words, there
has been a rip in the fabric of some relationship, and that
person understands that they need to mend the rip. Perhaps
a boundary has been unintentionally trespassed, and like
I've said before, a boundary is like a fence, and that fence
needs to be mended.

What exactly an amends looks like or sounds like depends on the person making it, and the person who is receiving it. What might restore or right a wrong for one person might need to be entirely different for someone else. But more often than not, a good amends is grounded in some obvious or concrete change of behavior in which certain words, deeds, or actions are performed or perhaps omitted.

24
Being happy rather than right all the time

24

Most folks are as happy as they make up their minds to be.
—Abraham Lincoln

Emotional intelligence equals happiness

The emotionally stunted person may demonstrate a tendency to try to be or appear "right" at everyone's expense, including their own. Perhaps you are familiar with the old saying, "They would cut off their nose to spite their face."

This is the person who has to win every argument, get in the last word, feel superior, or put people in their place. I worked with one man years ago who actually admitted to me in a consult that sometimes he would argue with his wife for hours, even if he knew she was right about something, until he wore her down and received an apology he was not due.

Do you know anyone who would rather be "right" than happy? This doesn't have to be you, because now you and your husband, lover, or partner are equipped to be a paragon of emotional health and well-being, able to express your feelings and emotions appropriately, and when you can't, you can apologize and make amends.

Congratulations on your continuing, deepening journey into intimacy and wholeness.

Printed in the USA
CPSIA information can be obtained
at www.ICGtesting.com
JSHW082212140824
68134JS00014B/580